CAT CONVERSATIONS

.

Renee Alter

Contents

Dedicated to Lampasas Community Cats—TNR,
who provided the cat house to provide a warm
place for cold nights

and my granddaughter Liliya.

Thank you, Francie Dailer, for your suggestions,
recommendations, and input on terminology.

Introduction

Once upon a time, there were some feral cats living on the bank of the creek behind the apartments where I moved to at the end of December 2015. They were multiplying, with new litters of kittens being born. Some of the kittens from different litters grew up together.

To stop animal control from catching them and bringing them to the animal shelter, I arranged to have seven TNRd (trapped, neutered, and released back where they were born) as soon as I learned someone I knew from Walmart got her 501(c)3 for Lampasas Community Cats—TNR. Many other communities have TNR programs, too. Wild cats can keep rodents, snakes, and most other cats away from the area you live in.

When the cats were returned to be released, one left the colony, two have crossed the rainbow bridge, one decided to live down the other end of the complex but still visits occasionally, and three remain as regular customers.

I took over providing them with water and nutritious food on my back patio. While they are completely feral (wild), keeping their distance once you open the door, they often peeked into my apartment through the glass storm door… even touching my hand when I place it on the glass… as long as there is glass between us.

This book is what occurs in my imagination when I observe their behavior. There are two males, littermates, I refer to as 'the boys.' I named the orange and white one Munchkin Pumpkin and the white one with a splash of tan Beautiful Boy aka Blue Eyes. Callie, a calico, aka Little Girl is the female from one of the other litters. I named the black and white one Oreo Cookie, Oreo for short. Little Mama, despite her size, had several litters of four before she was fixed.

Chapter 1

Rita was excited about being transferred into one of
the brand new remodeled apartments on the other
side of the complex from where she had been living
for four years. Once she got settled in, she noticed
there were lots of beautiful cats and kittens behind
the buildings on her end. Here is Little Mama with
Blue Eyes when he was just a kitten.

The neighbors were putting food out for them on
their back patios. The trouble was… the females,
including Little Mama, kept having more kittens.
When there were too many cats, some people called
animal control who brought traps, trapped them,

and took them away, even though some of us wanted to keep them all.

Little Mama, however, was very smart and stayed away from the traps. And she took really good care of her babies. When danger was near, she took them over the side of the hill to the bank of the creek where cat tails grew tall, and they could hide from humans. She took care of other kittens, too, including Callie. Blue Eyes, Munchkin, and Callie grew up and avoided being trapped, too.

One day, Rita saw on Facebook that Teri officially had a non-profit called Lampasas Community Cats—TNR. Rita took action. She contacted Teri and made pawprint earrings to sell to raise money to cover the expenses.

On the scheduled day, Teri's team brought regular traps plus a large drop-down trap. Rita talked to Earl about who would stay up all night to trap them… by pulling on a rope when one or more cats got under it. Earl said he is up most nights anyway. He would.

The idea of a drop-down trap was to hopefully catch a group of them eating at the same time. This didn't happen though. Teri, the TNR lady, gave Earl her phone number and said she would be up all night, too. Call her when they are trapped.

Earl did this… for each of the cats that were caught… including Little Mama and her charges. Teri came out each time Earl called to tell her he got one and transferred the trapped cat into a smaller trap, put a towel over it to help them feel safe, and moved it up onto Earl's patio. At dawn, there were seven.

Teri came in her Neuter Scooter and loaded up the seven cages. Paperwork was filled out for each cat and attached to each cage. Little Mama's family and the others were returned the day after their surgeries to recover overnight in Earl's apartment where it was safe and warm.

The next morning, with Rita and Earl looking on, each of the cages were opened one at a time to free the cats. It was beautiful sight to see as each of the cats ran off down the hill toward the creek bed… soon to return for the kibble that Earl put out on his patio. When feral cats are spayed and neutered as part of a TNR program, their left ears are harmlessly clipped to indicate they have been fixed and vaccinated. This avoids their getting trapped again.

Chapter 2

As Earl got older, it was harder for him to care for the cats, and Rita said she would take over. She brought a bowl of food over to Earl's, shook it to make noise, and walked slowly over to her unit with it. At first, the cats were confused, would begin to walk over, but then return to Earl's patio. It took many tries and a few days of coaxing, but they finally figured it out. Rita sighed with relief.

At first, Rita put the food out on her front patio, but some of the neighbors didn't like the cats and complained about them using their gardens for a litter box. Yes, they were using the dirt by Rita's front door as a litter box, too. And it didn't smell that great.

It was great news when the management company decided to redo the landscaping. Rita asked that the dirt in front of her unit be filled in with the same river rocks that other areas were being filled in with. She soon decided to move the feeding area to her back patio… which required some additional coaxing.

Once again, Rita shook the food dish and walked slowly to the back with it. Once again, the cats were confused. Once again, they finally figured it out. Rita sighed with relief.

Winter was coming, and Rita wanted to provide a warm place for the cats to go if they wanted to. She talked to Teri about different options. One day, Teri's team brought a wonderful cat house and filled it with straw.

The boys: "Look what they brought for us! Isn't it wonderful? We can hang out up on top as much as we want! It's a great spot for watching squirrels and birds."

Callie: "Aren't you going to go inside of it? That's what it is for…"

The boys: "Nah… we like it better up here."

Callie: "Suit yourself." And Callie proceeded to eat some kibble.

Chapter 3

Rita woke up with the sun and peeked out her bedroom window. Callie was waiting patiently inside the cat house and jumped out when she noticed the curtain move. She ran up to the window, excited her human was ready to put out food.

Callie: "You're awake! It's about time! I've been waiting here for hours!"

Not really, but Rita wondered if cats had any sense of time. She went to the kitchen to get fresh food to put out and opened the door. As always, Callie walked to the other side of the patio and turned her back as if she was embarrassed.

Rita: "Good morning Callie. It's good to see you!" She opened the storm door, poured food into two dishes, filled up the water bowl, and shut the door. Callie turned back around and returned to chow down some kibble. "Oh, Callie. What a silly girl!"

Within a short time, Blue Eyes poked his head around the corner and walked up onto the patio. Callie looked up and hissed, but he bashfully crept forward anyway to get some kibble from the second bowl. "Cool it, Callie. There's plenty for all of us."

Callie backed away. "Ewww. I don't want to eat at the same table as you…"

Munchkin arrived to join his brother. "Hey, Bro, be sure to leave plenty for me!"

Callie hissed at him, too. "I want to eat in private. Why can't you boys give me some privacy?"

Munchkin: "Oh… woah, girl! No offense! We all grew up together and have even shared the same food bowl. How come you don't like eating with us anymore?"

Callie backed off and sat by the outside closet door, dwelling on her mood. He was right. They used to all eat out of the same large bowl. All six of them when there were six. Maybe she is just getting old. Maybe she forgot why she got mad at them.

The boys finished their breakfast and lounged out on the patio in separate spots. Callie looked at each of them and cautiously crept forward even though she knew they've never been in a scuffle, and they posed no threats to her. Then she bolted for the entrance of the cat house she had claimed for her own and jumped inside to mope while the boys continued to lounge.

After the boys left and the coast was clear, Callie jumped out of the cat house to return to her daily routine.

That afternoon, Callie returned but the boys were on their way over, too, so she crouched down on the hill, hoping the boys wouldn't see her… and waited for them to leave.

Rita took a picture of her and said, "Silly girl. If I can see you, I'm sure the boys can see you, too!"

Chapter 4

One day, a new Tomcat appeared on the grounds competing for the food source. Rita named him Bully Boy. Each time the three cats saw him, they bolted… and he took off after them to try and run them down. It was scary for Rita to watch as she worried about her little charges. Back on the patio, the boys had returned and were reminiscing.

Munchkin: "Gee, Bro. Callie used to be our friend. Do you think we did something wrong? She doesn't seem to like us anymore. I hope she doesn't stay mad at us forever."

Blue Eyes: "Yeh, I noticed. We always leave her kibble. Maybe she is holding a grudge because we didn't protect her from Bully Boy. Although, I would think that getting him to chase me in another direction would keep him away from her."

Munchkin: "Yeh, maybe because we didn't protect her, she got mean to run him off herself and doesn't know how to turn the mean off."

Blue Eyes: "Too bad. She just doesn't know how to have fun anymore."

Munchkin: "Bully Boy is so intimidating. I panic and run every time I see him. When he first showed up, I thought he was going to kill me! I ran straight up the side of the tree!"

Blue Eyes: "I thought he was going to kill me, too! Have you seen the hissy fit Callie has when he comes toward her now? And he even backs down? She used to run, too!"

Munchkin: "Bully Boy hasn't been as aggressive lately. He doesn't chase us anymore. But I still panic and bolt when I see him. I feel like such a coward."

Blue Eyes: "Oh, don't feel so bad. Me, too!"

Chapter 5

Soon, the boys decided to go exploring. It was Spring. Between birds, squirrels, butterflies, moths, wasps, lizards, ants, and other critters, there was plenty of eye candy to keep them occupied. That afternoon, they each found somewhere to take a nap.

After their nap, the boys saw their favorite human come to the door and began approaching her with their heads together. You might think they were Siamese twins. Maybe Blue Eyes was part Siamese.

Rita saw their adorable behavior and began talking to them. "Hello, boys! It's good to see you! I love it when you come over to visit me!"

"Aren't we just the cutest cats in the neighborhood?" the boys said together.

Rita: "You're so cute!"

The boys: "Yes, we sure are!"

The boys came up to the storm door, got up on their hind legs, and looked through the glass. "You humans live in strange places. Where are the trees and flowers? We don't see any. There isn't even any dirt." After the boys looked around for a few minutes, they jumped down and walked away.

It was like groundhog day for the cats. Each day, they did the same things… walk around on the same route, count the same cars, watch all the wild critters, and look through the glass of the storm door when the inside door was open and wonder why humans live in strange places.

Chapter 6

While Callie claimed the inside of the cat house, Munchkin claimed the top. Sometimes he napped on the stones near the flowers, but mostly, he napped on top of the cat house. The boys used to nap together, but lately they have been napping in separate places close to Rita's unit.

Munchkin: "I love our human. I can tell she really loves us, too. This is my favorite place to hang out these days."

Blue Eyes: "I love our human, too. Sometimes, I think about bringing her presents. She keeps looking out the windows to see what we are doing. I like looking cute so she will take pictures of us. Look! She is smiling at us again!"

Munchkin: "Yes, she is. But I see a new moving machine I want to investigate."

Blue Eyes: "OK. This is the one the human who comes to visit Rita uses."

The boys walked under the Nissan pickup truck to start their investigation, sniffing every inch of the underside carriage.

Munchkin: "Mmmm. It's smells like our species. Doesn't it?"

Blue Eyes: "Most definitely. And a lot more than one."

Munchkin: "I hope they aren't coming over to eat up all our kibble."

Blue Eyes: "If any of them do, we can chase them off… I mean run…"

Munchkin: "Na-nah-nah-nah-nah… you can't run up trees like I can."

Blue Eyes: "Don't rub it in."

Munchkin: "Okay. I'll be nice."

Blue Eyes: "I'm going to go down to the creek now to see if I can find any frogs."

Munchkin: "Okay, I know I just took a nap, but I am ready to take another one."

Rita felt the same way. She moseyed into her bedroom to take an afternoon nap.

Chapter 7

Even though Callie hissed at the boys every time they approached her, they still approached… but slowly with much caution. They never knew what kind of mood she was going to be in.

Sometimes, Callie surprised the boys by butting her forehead with theirs, but they didn't trust her intentions. It was more like a shock than a forehead touch, and they squinched and backed away just a tad.

Callie: "Hi, guys! Good to see you!"

Munchkin: "Yeh… good to see you, too! What's up? Why are you suddenly acting friendly?"

Callie: "No particular reason, I guess."

Munchkin was even more surprised when Callie was willing to eat out of the same dish as him. He looked at her out of the corner of his eye, not quite trusting how friendly she was behaving. In a split second, she could go from friendly to hissing. Just then, Blue Eyes came up from behind her and nipped her on her butt.

Callie: "Yeowww!"

Callie bolted into the cat house. Gee, no wonder she was so irritated with them.

The boys peeked in through the glass. "Hey human, it's raining out here! Did you notice? We'll just hang out here by your front door where it is dry."

Since the boys seemed to hang out close to Rita's apartment so much, she decided to prop open her storm door to see if either of them wanted to come in. After all, it was raining outside.

Blue Eyes walked in just past the door jamb to look around. His sidekick, Munchkin, stretched his neck to look over his brother but backed away. He wasn't as brave as his brother was.

Blue Eyes' curiosity got the better of him, and he continued to walk in and explore more of the apartment. He looked into various places, mostly at containers that had stuff in them. Then he ventured further and looked into the bedroom. Then the bathroom. Munchkin was waiting for him when he went back outside.

Munchkin: "Well, what did you see?"

Blue Eyes: "I saw the human… and a lot of strange-looking useless stuff in boxes. But it also looks like she has everything she needs… there's a large bed to sleep on, a flushable litter box, and removable fur to put on when it gets cold. I also saw toys, imaging screens, books, and writing sticks.

"At least there were a few plants. You should come in with me some time to look for yourself. Maybe with both of us together, it will feel less scary. But I really do like it better out here."

Munchkin: "I like it better when we're together. Will you promise me you'll never leave me?"

Blue Eyes: "I can't completely promise, but I'll do my best."

Blue Eyes: "I didn't see any evidence that our human has a cat that lives inside. We must be special. There are other humans that are nice to us, but this one is extra nice."

Munchkin: "The other humans go outside a lot and drive in those big machines. Our human hardly EVER comes out. She just watches us through the glass."

Blue Eyes: "Yes, I noticed that, too. But we can always count on her to feed us!"

Munchkin: "That's for sure! And another human comes over almost every day. I like the one called Jesyka. I heard her say she has FOURTEEN cats!"

Blue Eyes: "I can even smell them on the bottom of her driving machine. That's how I knew she was an ally."

Chapter 8

Sometimes, other guests arrive by the back door. One day, when Rita opened the door, she saw a small opossum eating out of the cat dish when the others were off somewhere else. Due to his size, he must have been a baby… with a huge appetite.

Rita: "Hey, Possum, where did you come from? You're not a cat!"

Possum: "Crunch, crunch, crunch."

Possum didn't answer. He thought that maybe if he didn't say anything, the human wouldn't notice him.

Rita: "Where do you live?"

Possum: "Crunch, crunch, crunch."

Rita: "Where's your family?"

Possum: "Crunch, crunch, crunch."

Rita gave up getting an answer from Possum and walked away. Possum ate until he was full and sauntered away.

Later, the game camera sent an alert. Rita opened the app on her phone to see the three regulars… with Callie looking out from inside the house! She snapped a photo quick! Callie is so silly!

Another day, Callie was the first one to arrive for breakfast. Blue Eyes walked up behind her, and soon Munchkin followed. When Callie realized the boys were there, she jumped, darted around them, and jumped inside the house again.

Another day, Rita opened the door to find Oreo eating. It had been a long time since she had seen her.

Rita: "Oreo, hello! How are you? What brings you down this end today?"

Oreo: "Oh, hi, Rita. Raynell didn't put out food today. I think she went somewhere. I remembered you and came down to see if you had any. I'm so glad you did… I was really hungry!'

Then Munchkin arrived.

Munchkin: "Hi Oreo! You're still as cute as you ever were… and you didn't hiss at me. Callie is mad at us and hisses whenever she sees us. Where have you been?"

Oreo: "Oh, dear. I'm sorry to hear about Callie. Raynell is deaf and needed me, so I stay down there to keep her company. She has an inside cat that never comes outside and just looks out the window."

Munchkin: "Well, don't be a stranger. Come down to visit any time."

Oreo: "Why, thank you! I look forward to doing that."

In case you haven't noticed yet, the tip of the left ears of feral cats are snipped to mark that they have been TNRd. You can see this clearly on Oreo.

Chapter 9

Rita went for a walk one day and came across this scene in the next parking area. She overheard the following conversation between the cats.

Blue Eyes: "My, it's a hot day. I will sit under this car to get some shade. Hey, Munchkin! Come over and sit with me."

Munchkin: "Nah, I'd rather sit under this other car instead. I like this car better."

Oreo: "What are you guys doing?"

Blue Eyes: "Sitting under cars for some shade."

Oreo: "Cool. I'll sit under this one."

Little Mama: "My word. I suppose there are enough cars for everyone. Might as well take advantage of the situation. I'll sit under this one."

Blue Eyes: "Mama… isn't it a nice day today?"

Little Mama: "Yes, son. Very nice. I find it hard to believe, though, that each of you want your own car. It would be more economical if you share one."

Munchkin: "I suppose. But this IS way more fun."

Oreo: "For sure. Besides, all the humans are staying inside today. It's too hot out here for them."

Blue Eyes: "Humans need their air conditioning."

Munchkin: "Humans make a lot of trash, too. Then they have to put it in the dumpster. And a big truck comes to pick it up."

Oreo: "That's why we are safe sitting under these cars."

Blue Eyes: "If the humans left the dumpster open, I'd go treasure hunting. They often throw perfectly good food away."

Munchkin: "Yes, they do. I remember when I found some fish sticks from McDonald's."

Oreo: "I remember when I found a burger from Burger King."

Little Mama: "Boys and girls, you must be careful if you go into a dumpster. If a human closes the top while you are in there, who knows when you'll be able to get out again."

Blue Eyes: "Yes, mama. We'll be good."

Munchkin: "You all are making me hungry. I'm going over to Rita's to get some kibble."

Oreo: "Me, too!"

Blue Eyes: "I'll follow you."

Little Mama: "Bye children. I'm going down into the creek to hunt some REAL food."

About the Author

Renee Alter is an author, poet, storyteller, health nut, and volunteers in her community. Her hobbies include writing, blogging, creating books, photography, continuous education on a variety of topics, networking, songwriting, and music. She now resides in Central Texas.

Other Books by Renee Alter

Appearances: A Journey of Self-Discovery

Reflections: A Toolbox of Poetry

Love, Life, & God: Getting Past the Pain

View From A Tree

Creating A Meaningful Life After Disability: Posts From My Blog

Blog Therapy: Posts From My Blog Part 2

Miracles Sandwiched Between the Challenges: Making It Through The Roller Coasters Of My Life With The Help Of My Guardian Angels (Short Story)

Growing An Internal Garden to Cope With Chronic Pain, Illness, & Depression

Alternative Realities: Daydreams of Conversations

The Land of Mark (Short Story-Kindle & Audible)

The Adventures of Gnat (Short Story-Kindle & Audible)

Twin Flame (Short Story-Kindle & Audible)

Blogging A Path To The Future: Posts From My Blog Part 3

Living With Symptomatic Spondylolisthesis

Lessons From Nature: Poetry, Prose, & Photography

On the Move: Autobiography of a Survivor

Metamorphosis: Posts From My Blog Part 4

I hope you enjoyed this little book about the cat colony I take care of. As of the publication of this book, paw print earrings are still available for sale. 100% of the proceeds goes to LCC-LLC. Send your request via the Blogger Contact Form on reneealtersatmosphere.blogspot.com.

Please share and leave a review on Amazon.
www.amazon.com/author/reneealter